MW01248346

# DAD JOKES

## THE BEST KIND OF JOKES IN EXISTENCE

WHAT DO YOU CALL A LINE OF MEN
WAITING TO GET HAIRCUTS?

A BARBERQUEUE.

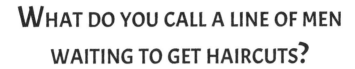

WHAT KIND OF TEACHER NEVER FARTS
IN PUBLIC?

A PRIVATE TOOTER.

I WENT TO A NEW MECHANIC.

THEY CAME HIGHLY WRECK-A-MENDED.

I ASKED MY WIFE WHICH ONE SHE LIKED
BETTER, MY FACE OR MY BODY?

SHE SAID, "YOUR SENSE OF HUMOR."

MY WIFE ASKED ME WHAT WOULD STOP
THE STAIRS FROM CREAKING..

APPARENTLY "WEIGHT WATCHERS"
WAS NOT THE RIGHT ANSWER.

DAD, CAN YOU TELL ME WHAT A SOLAR
ECLIPSE IS?

NO SUN.

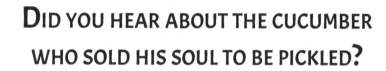

DID YOU HEAR ABOUT THE CUCUMBER WHO SOLD HIS SOUL TO BE PICKLED?

HE MADE A DILL WITH THE DEVIL.

LADIES, IF HE CAN'T APPRECIATE YOUR FRUIT JOKES,

YOU NEED TO LET THAT MANGO.

WHAT'S THE DIFFERENCE BETWEEN A
HIPPO AND A ZIPPO?

ONE IS REALLY HEAVY AND THE OTHER
IS A LITTLE LIGHTER.

I WOULD MAKE JOKES ABOUT THE SEA,

BUT THEY'RE TOO DEEP.

WHAT'S THE CLEANEST TYPE OF MUSIC?

A SOAP OPERA.

TOOK MY WIFE TO A VINEYARD TODAY.

ALL SHE DID WAS WHINE.

GHOSTS ARE ALWAYS WILLING TO TELL YOU EVERYTHING.

BECAUSE OF THEIR TRANSPARENCY.

MY WIFE ASKED IF I'VE SEEN THE DOG BOWL.

I SAID I NEVER KNEW HE DID!

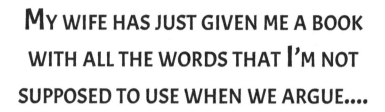

MY WIFE HAS JUST GIVEN ME A BOOK WITH ALL THE WORDS THAT I'M NOT SUPPOSED TO USE WHEN WE ARGUE....

IT'S CALLED A DICTIONARY.

I'VE BEEN LISTENING TO A LOT OF NATIONAL ANTHEMS.

I LOVE COUNTRY MUSIC.

I'M GOING TO TRY VELCRO INSTEAD OF SHOE LACES.

WHY KNOT?

MY KID SWALLOWED SOME COINS, THE DOCTOR TOLD ME TO JUST WAIT.

NO CHANGE YET.

WHEN IS A DOOR NOT A DOOR?

WHEN IT'S AJAR.

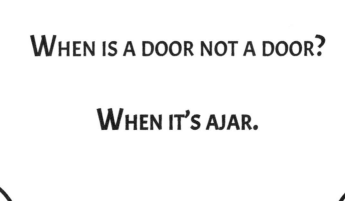

WHAT DO YOU CALL AN ANGRY
CARROT?

A STEAMED VEGGIE.

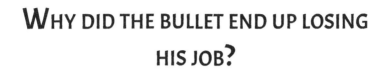

W**HY DID THE BULLET END UP LOSING HIS JOB?**

H**E GOT FIRED.**

W**HAT DO YOU CALL THE GHOST OF A CHICKEN?**

A **POULTRY-GEIST.**

**W**HAT DO YOU CALL TWO GHOSTS
HAVING AN ARGUMENT?

**A** SPIRITED DEBATE.

**M**Y WIFE LIKES MY **D**AD JOKES.

**S**HE'S A GROAN WOMAN.

MY WIFE PREFERS TO TAKE THE STAIRS, BUT I ALWAYS TAKE THE ELEVATOR.

I GUESS WE WERE JUST RAISED DIFFERENTLY.

WHAT VEGETABLE SHOULD YOU NEVER BRING ON A BOAT?

A LEEK.

I ONCE GOT FIRED FROM A CANNED JUICE FACTORY.

APPARENTLY, I COULDN'T CONCENTRATE.

WHAT DO YOU CALL A TYPO ON A HEADSTONE?

A GRAVE MISTAKE.

IF SWEET DREAMS ARE MADE OF CHEESE

WHO AM I TO DIS-A-BRIE?

WHAT DOES A PAINTER DO WHEN HE GETS COLD?

PUTS ON ANOTHER COAT.

WHEN DOES A JOKE BECOME A "DAD JOKE"?

WHEN IT BECOMES APPARENT.

WHY DIDN'T HAN SOLO ENJOY HIS STEAK DINNER?

IT WAS CHEWIE.

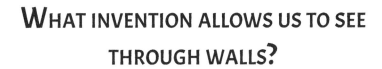

WHAT INVENTION ALLOWS US TO SEE THROUGH WALLS?

WINDOWS.

WHAT DO YOU CALL IT WHEN A GROUP OF APES STARTS A COMPANY?

MONKEY BUSINESS.

HOW DO YOU MAKE HOLY WATER?

YOU BOIL THE HELL OUT OF IT.

HOW DO YOU TELL THE DIFFERENCE BETWEEN AN ALLIGATOR AND A CROCODILE?

YOU WILL SEE ONE LATER AND ONE IN A WHILE.

I'M AN EXPERT AT PICKING LEAVES AND
HEATING THEM IN WATER.

IT'S MY SPECIAL TEA.

WHY DON'T PIRATES TAKE A BATH
BEFORE THEY WALK THE PLANK?

THEY JUST WASH UP ON SHORE.

**W**HAT DID THE **F**RENCH CHEF GIVE HIS WIFE FOR **V**ALENTINE'S **D**AY?

**A** HUG AND A QUICHE.

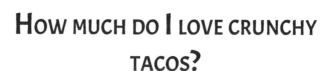

**H**OW MUCH DO **I** LOVE CRUNCHY TACOS?

**F**ROM MY HEAD TOMATOES.

WHAT HAPPENS WHEN A SNOWMAN THROWS A TANTRUM?

HE HAS A MELTDOWN.

WHAT KEY IS USED TO OPEN BANANAS?

A MON-KEY.

# WHAT DO YOU CALL TWO OCTOPUSES THAT LOOK THE SAME?

## ITENTICLE.

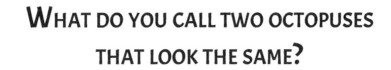

I TOLD MY WIFE SHE NEEDS TO START EMBRACING HER MISTAKES.

## SO, SHE HUGGED ME.

WHAT DO YOU CALL A VAPING
VAMPIRE?

VLAD THE INHALER.

HOW DO YOU MEASURE THE QUALITY
OF A DAD JOKE?

WITH A SIGHSMOGRAPH.

## WHAT'S A GHOST LEAST FAVORITE ROOM OF YOUR HOUSE?

THE "LIVING" ROOM.

## WHAT DID ONE DNA SAY TO THE OTHER DNA?

"DO THESE GENES MAKE ME LOOK FAT?"

WHY ARE ELEVATOR JOKES SO CLASSIC AND GOOD?

THEY WORK ON MANY LEVELS.

TWO GUYS WALKED INTO A BAR.

THE THIRD GUY DUCKED.

DID YOU HEAR ABOUT THE
RESTAURANT ON THE MOON?

GREAT FOOD, NO ATMOSPHERE.

WHAT DO YOU CALL TWO MONKEYS
WHO SHARE AN AMAZON PRIME
ACCOUNT?

PRIME MATES.

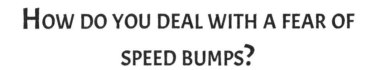

How do you deal with a fear of speed bumps?

You slowly get over it.

What do you call a fancy fish?

So-fish-ticated.

I'M WORRIED FOR THE CALENDAR.

ITS DAYS ARE NUMBERED.

WHAT DID THE BUFFALO SAY TO ITS SON WHEN HE LEFT?

BISON!

I HAVE A CLEAN CONSCIENCE

—IT'S NEVER BEEN USED.

WHY DIDN'T THE ASTRONAUT COME
HOME TO HIS WIFE?

HE NEEDED HIS SPACE.

WHAT'S THE BEST AIR TO BREATHE IF
YOU WANT TO BE RICH?

MILLIONAIRE.

WHAT'S A LAWYER'S FAVORITE DRINK?

SUBPOENA COLADA.

HOW DOES AN ATTORNEY SLEEP?

FIRST, HE LIES ON ONE SIDE, THEN HE LIES ON THE OTHER.

WHAT DO APPLES DO AT THE GYM?

A CORE WORKOUT.

WHY DO THE FRENCH LOVE SNAILS?

BECAUSE THEY DON'T EAT FAST FOOD!

WHAT ARE WINDMILLS' FAVORITE GENRE OF MUSIC?

THEY'RE BIG METAL FANS.

I WROTE A SONG FOR A TORTILLA.

WELL, IT'S MORE OF A WRAP.

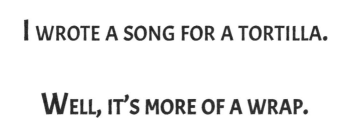

WHY DO BANANAS WEAR SUNSCREEN?

BECAUSE THEY PEEL.

**W**HY CAN'T THE SAILOR LEARN THE ALPHABET?

**B**ECAUSE HE KEPT GETTING LOST AT **C.**

**I** CAN ALWAYS TELL WHEN MY WIFE IS LYING JUST BY LOOKING AT HER.

**I** CAN ALSO TELL WHEN SHE'S STANDING.

AN APPLE A DAY KEEPS THE DOCTOR AWAY.

AT LEAST IT DOES IF YOU THROW IT HARD ENOUGH.

WHAT DO YOU CALL A FRENCHMAN WEARING SANDALS?

PHILIPPE FLOP.

## WHAT HAPPENS WHEN DOCTORS GET FRUSTRATED?

## THEY LOSE THEIR PATIENTS.

## WHY DON'T EGGS TELL JOKES?

## THEY'D CRACK EACH OTHER UP.

**WHAT DO COWS LIKE TO READ?**

**CATTLE-LOGS.**

**WHY IS IT SO CHEAP TO THROW A PARTY AT A HAUNTED HOUSE?**

**BECAUSE THE GHOSTS BRING ALL THE BOOS.**

ALL VAMPIRES KEEP THEIR MONEY IN A SPECIAL PLACE

— THE BLOOD BANK.

WHY ARE SPIDERS SO SMART?

THEY CAN FIND EVERYTHING ON THE WEB.

**WHAT DID BENJAMIN FRANKLIN SAY WHEN HE DISCOVERED ELECTRICITY?**

**NOTHING. HE WAS TOO SHOCKED.**

**WHEN DO COMPUTERS OVERHEAT?**

**WHEN THEY NEED TO VENT.**

## WHAT IS THE PERIODIC TABLE CALLED ON HALLOWEEN?

### THE ATOMS FAMILY!

## I PLAY THE WORLD'S MOST DANGEROUS SPORT.

### I DISAGREE WITH MY WIFE.

WHAT DO YOU CALL SOMEONE WHO CAN'T STICK TO A DIET?

A DESSERTER.

THE BEST GIFT I EVER RECEIVED WAS A BROKEN DRUM.

YOU CAN'T BEAT THAT.

WHAT DID THE BLANKET SAY TO THE BED?

I'VE GOT YOU COVERED.

WHAT DID THE SEAL WITH ONE FIN SAY TO THE SHARK?

IF SEAL IS BROKEN, DO NOT CONSUME.

Wʜʏ ᴅɪᴅ ᴛʜᴇ ʙᴀɴᴀɴᴀ ɢᴏ ᴛᴏ ᴛʜᴇ ᴅᴏᴄᴛᴏʀ?

Iᴛ ᴡᴀsɴ'ᴛ ᴘᴇᴇʟɪɴɢ ᴡᴇʟʟ.

Hᴏᴡ ᴅᴏᴇs ᴛʜᴇ ʀᴀɴᴄʜᴇʀ ᴋᴇᴇᴘ ᴛʀᴀᴄᴋ ᴏғ ʜɪs ᴄᴀᴛᴛʟᴇ?

Wɪᴛʜ ᴀ ᴄᴏᴡ-ᴄᴜʟᴀᴛᴏʀ.

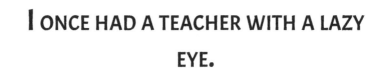

I ONCE HAD A TEACHER WITH A LAZY EYE.

SHE COULDN'T CONTROL HER PUPILS.

HOW DOES A PENGUIN BUILD A HOUSE?

IGLOOS IT TOGETHER.

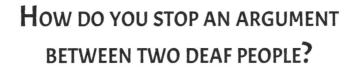

HOW DO YOU STOP AN ARGUMENT
BETWEEN TWO DEAF PEOPLE?

TURN THE LIGHTS OFF.

WHAT DO YOU CALL A HERD OF SHEEP
FALLING DOWN A HILL?

A LAMBSLIDE.

WHY CAN'T A LEOPARD HIDE?

BECAUSE HE'S ALWAYS SPOTTED.

HOW DO TREES GET ON THE INTERNET?

THEY LOG IN.

**WHAT KIND OF MUSIC SHOULD YOU LISTEN TO WHILE FISHING?**

**SOMETHING CATCHY!**

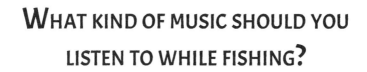

**WHAT KIND OF FRUIT DO GHOSTS LIKE?**

**BOO-BERRIES.**

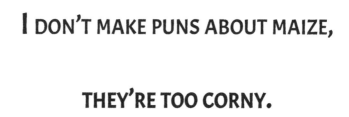

I DON'T MAKE PUNS ABOUT MAIZE,

THEY'RE TOO CORNY.

THE FIRST RULE OF THE PASSIVE-AGGRESSIVE CLUB IS . . .

WELL, NEVER MIND. YOU WOULDN'T UNDERSTAND IT ANYWAY.

IF TWO VEGETARIANS GET IN AN ARGUMENT,

IS IT STILL CALLED BEEF?

WHERE DO DADS STORE THEIR DAD JOKES?

IN THE DAD-A-BASE.

# What's a scarecrow's favorite fruit?

## Straw-berries.

# How do cows stay up to date?

## They read the Moo-spaper.

WHAT DO YOU GIVE A SICK LEMON?

LEMON-AID.

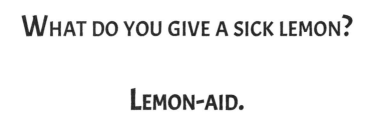

WHY DID THE EMPLOYEE GET FIRED FROM THE KEYBOARD FACTORY?

HE WASN'T PUTTING IN ENOUGH SHIFTS.

WHY ARE TEDDY BEARS NEVER HUNGRY?

THEY ARE ALWAYS STUFFED!

WHAT'S THE MOST IMPORTANT PART OF A MAILMAN JOKE?

THE DELIVERY.

## WHAT DID THE FLOWERS DO WHEN THE BRIDE WALKED DOWN THE AISLE?

### THEY ROSE.

## THE PAST, THE PRESENT, AND THE FUTURE WALKED INTO A BAR.

### IT WAS TENSE.

CAN FEBRUARY MARCH?

NO, BUT APRIL MAY.

WHY WAS THE BROOM LATE TO CLASS?

IT OVER-SWEPT.

NOT SURE IF YOU HAVE NOTICED, BUT I LOVE BAD PUNS.

THAT'S JUST HOW EYE ROLL.

SINGING IN THE SHOWER IS FUN UNTIL YOU GET SOAP IN YOUR MOUTH.

THEN IT BECOMES A SOAP OPERA.

WHAT DID THE SINK TELL THE TOILET?

YOU LOOK FLUSHED!

WHAT DO YOU CALL A COW WITH NO LEGS?

GROUND BEEF.

HOW DOES A LAWYER SAY GOODBYE?

I'LL BE SUING YA!

WHAT DID ONE PLATE SAY TO ANOTHER PLATE?

TONIGHT, DINNER'S ON ME.

**WHAT IS THE EASTER BUNNY'S FAVORITE TYPE OF MUSIC?**

**HIP-HOP.**

**CAN I DIVE IN THIS POOL?**

**IT DEEP-ENDS.**

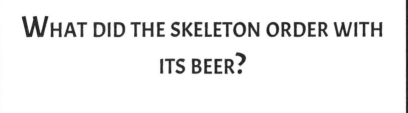

## WHAT DID THE SKELETON ORDER WITH ITS BEER?

### A MOP.

## WHERE DID THE CAT GO AFTER LOSING ITS TAIL?

### THE RETAIL STORE.

WHY ARE CEMETERIES ALWAYS FENCED OFF?

BECAUSE EVERYONE IS JUST DYING TO GET IN.

WHAT WOULD HAPPEN IF THE UNIVERSE EXPLODED?

NO MATTER.

## WHAT KIND OF JEWELRY DO RABBITS WEAR?

**14 CARROT GOLD.**

## WHERE DO PIRATES GET THEIR HOOKS?

**SECOND HAND STORES.**

**WHAT DID THE BABY CORN SAY TO THE MAMA CORN?**

**WHERE'S POPCORN?**

**WHAT DO YOU CALL A LAZY KANGAROO?**

**POUCH POTATO.**

SCIENTISTS HAVE DISCOVERED WHAT IS BELIEVED TO BE THE WORLD'S LARGEST BEDSHEET.

MORE ON THIS STORY AS IT UNFOLDS.

WHY IS IT A BAD IDEA TO EAT A CLOCK?

BECAUSE IT'S SO TIME-CONSUMING.

WHERE DO BURGERS GO DANCING?

AT THE MEATBALL.

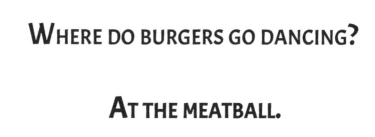

WHY DID THE SPOON COME TO THE PARTY DRESSED AS A KNIFE?

THE INVITATION SAID TO LOOK SHARP.

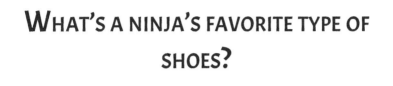

# What's a ninja's favorite type of shoes?

## Sneakers!

# What's a vampire's favorite ship?

## A blood vessel.

"I HAVE A SPLIT PERSONALITY," SAID TOM,

BEING FRANK.

DID YOU HEAR THE RUMOR ABOUT BUTTER?

WELL, I'M NOT GOING TO SPREAD IT!

## What kind of sandals do frogs wear?

### Open-toad.

## Police arrested a bottle of water because it was wanted in three different states:

### Solid, liquid, and gas.

I DON'T TRUST STAIRS.

THEY ARE ALWAYS UP TO SOMETHING.

WHAT'S THE DIFFERENCE BETWEEN A PIANO, A CAN OF TUNA AND A GLUE STICK?

YOU CAN TUNA PIANO, BUT YOU CAN'T PIANO A TUNA.

**WHAT KIND OF DOCTOR IS DR. PEPPER?**

**A FIZZICIAN.**

**HOW DID THE BARBER WIN THE RACE?**

**HE KNEW A SHORTCUT.**

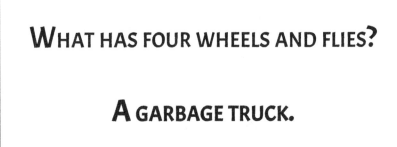

**W**HAT HAS FOUR WHEELS AND FLIES?

**A** GARBAGE TRUCK.

**T**HERE'S ONLY ONE THING **I** CAN'T DEAL WITH,

AND THAT'S A DECK OF CARDS GLUED TOGETHER.

WHY DO VAMPIRES ALWAYS SEEM SICK?

THEY'RE COFFIN.

WHAT'S MORE UNBELIEVABLE THAN A TALKING DOG?

A SPELLING BEE.

JUST PAID **$200** FOR A BELT THAT DOESN'T FIT!

WHAT A HUGE WAIST!

WHAT DID THE VOLCANO SAY TO HIS WIFE?

I LAVA YOU.

WHY WAS THE COMPUTER LATE FOR WORK?

IT HAD A HARD DRIVE.

WHAT DO YOU CALL BIRDS THAT STICK TOGETHER?

VELCROWS.

**WHAT DO YOU CALL A SLEEPING BULL?**

**A BULLDOZER.**

**WHY IS GRASS SO DANGEROUS?**

**BECAUSE IT'S FULL OF BLADES.**

**W**HAT DID THE POLICE OFFICER SAY TO HIS BELLY-BUTTON?

**Y**OU'RE UNDER A VEST.

**H**OW MANY NARCISSISTS DOES IT TAKE TO SCREW IN A LIGHT BULB?

**O**NE. **T**HE NARCISSIST HOLDS THE LIGHT BULB WHILE THE REST OF THE WORLD REVOLVES AROUND HIM.

WHY DID THE HIPSTER BURN HIS MOUTH ON PIZZA?

BECAUSE HE ATE IT BEFORE IT WAS COOL.

BECOMING VEGETARIAN WAS A HUGE

MISSED STEAK.

WHAT DO YOU CALL A LAWYER WHO CAN COOK?

A SUE CHEF.

COFFEE HAS A ROUGH TIME IN OUR HOUSE.

IT GETS MUGGED EVERY SINGLE MORNING!

HOW DOES A VAMPIRE START A LETTER?

TOMB IT MAY CONCERN!

WHAT IS WORSE THAN FINDING A
WORM IN YOUR APPLE?

FINDING HALF A WORM.

SWORDS WILL NEVER GO OBSOLETE.

THEY'RE CUTTING EDGE TECHNOLOGY.

WHAT DO YOU CALL A PIG THAT DOES KARATE?

PORK CHOP.

DID YOU HEAR ABOUT THE SALE ON PADDLES?

IT WAS QUITE THE OAR-DEAL.

DON'T SPELL PART BACKWARDS.

IT'S A TRAP.

THE ADJECTIVE FOR METAL IS METALLIC,

BUT NOT SO FOR IRON WHICH IS IRONIC.

WHAT HAPPENS WHEN IT RAINS CATS AND DOGS?

YOU HAVE TO BE CAREFUL NOT TO STEP IN A POODLE.

I REFUSE TO WORK WITH COMPOST,

IT'S DEGRADING.

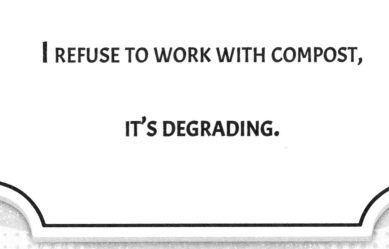

PIGS ARE NO FUN TO HANG AROUND.

THEY'RE JUST A BOAR.

**WHAT DO YOU CALL THE SECURITY OUTSIDE OF A SAMSUNG STORE?**

**GUARDIANS OF THE GALAXY.**

**JOKES ABOUT GERMAN SAUSAGE ARE**

**THE WURST.**

I FIRED THE GUY I HIRED TO MOW MY LAWN.

HE JUST DIDN'T CUT IT.

WHAT'S THE LEAST SPOKEN LANGUAGE IN THE WORLD?

SIGN LANGUAGE.

I STAYED UP ALL NIGHT TO SEE WHERE THE SUN WENT.

THEN IT DAWNED ON ME.

WHAT DO YOU CALL AN ALLIGATOR IN A VEST?

AN INVESTIGATOR.

I CHANGED MY PHONE'S NAME TO TITANIC.

IT'S SYNCING NOW.

WHY DID THE ACTOR FALL THROUGH THE FLOORBOARDS?

HE WAS GOING THROUGH A STAGE!

**W**HAT DO YOU CALL A BROKEN CAN OPENER?

**A** CAN'T OPENER.

**I** TRIED TO START A PROFESSIONAL HIDE AND SEEK TEAM, BUT IT DIDN'T WORK OUT.

**T**URNS OUT, GOOD PLAYERS ARE HARD TO FIND.

**W**HY DO TEENAGE GIRLS TRAVEL IN ODD NUMBERED GROUPS?

**B**ECAUSE THEY JUST CAN'T EVEN.

**W**HAT HAPPENED WHEN THE WORLD'S TONGUE-TWISTER CHAMPION GOT ARRESTED?

**T**HEY GAVE HIM A TOUGH SENTENCE!

My boss is going to fire the employee with the worst posture.

I have a hunch, it might be me.

Which bear is the most condescending?

A pan-duh!

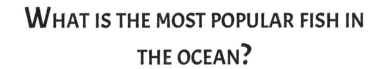

**WHAT IS THE MOST POPULAR FISH IN THE OCEAN?**

**A STARFISH.**

**WHAT DO YOU CALL PEOPLE WHO ARE AFRAID OF SANTA CLAUS?**

**CLAUSTROPHOBIC.**

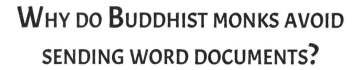

WHY DO BUDDHIST MONKS AVOID SENDING WORD DOCUMENTS?

THEY'RE SUPPOSED TO AVOID ATTACHMENTS.

WHAT DO YOU CALL A MEDIEVAL LAMP?

A KNIGHT LIGHT.

WHAT IS THE FASTEST GROWING CITY IN THE WORLD?

CAPITAL OF IRELAND. IT'S DUBLIN EVERYDAY.

WHY ARE OYSTERS GREEDY?

BECAUSE THEY'RE SHELLFISH.

BREAD IS A LOT LIKE THE SUN.

IT RISES IN THE YEAST AND SETS IN THE WAIST.

WHAT DO YOU CALL A PRISONER GOING DOWN THE STAIRS?

A CON-DESCENDING.

NOT ALL MATH PUNS ARE TERRIBLE.

JUST SUM.

WHAT DO YOU CALL A COW WITH A TWITCH?

BEEF JERKY.

**W**HAT DO YOU CALL A FISH WEARING A BOW TIE?

**S**OFISHTICATED.

**W**HICH DAY DO POTATOES FEAR THE MOST?

**F**RYDAY.

WHY WAS KING ARTHUR'S ARMY TOO TIRED TO FIGHT?

BECAUSE OF ALL THOSE SLEEPLESS KNIGHTS.

WHY DID THE COFFEE SHOP CLOSE FOR THE DAY?

BECAUSE A STORM WAS BREWING.

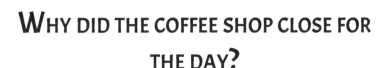

WILL GLASS COFFINS BE A SUCCESS?

REMAINS TO BE SEEN.

WHAT'S AN ASTRONAUT'S FAVORITE PART OF A COMPUTER?

THE SPACE BAR.

WHY ARE SKELETONS SO CALM?

BECAUSE NOTHING GETS UNDER THEIR SKIN.

I'VE STARTED TELLING EVERYONE ABOUT THE BENEFITS OF EATING DRIED GRAPES.

IT'S ALL ABOUT RAISIN AWARENESS.

**W**HY DID THE CANDLE QUIT HIS JOB?

**H**E WAS BURNED OUT.

**O**NE BIRD CAN'T MAKE A PUN.

**B**UT TOUCAN.

WHAT BUILDING HAS THE MOST STORIES?

THE LIBRARY.

WHAT KIND OF CATS LIKE TO GO BOWLING?

ALLEY CATS.

THIS MAY SOUND BANANAS BUT

I FIND YOU A-PEELING.

WHAT DO YOU CALL A COW WHO'S
JUST GIVEN BIRTH?

DE-CALF-INATED.

**WHAT ARE TEN THINGS YOU CAN ALWAYS COUNT ON?**

**YOUR FINGERS.**

**HOW MUCH DOES A HIPSTER WEIGH?**

**AN INSTAGRAM.**

Made in the USA
Monee, IL
06 December 2022

19907159R00059